ADVENTURES IN THE
GREAT OUTDOORS

HUNTING

ROBYN
HARDYMAN

WINDMILL
BOOKS

New York

Published in 2014 by Windmill Books, An Imprint of Rosen Publishing
29 East 21st Street, New York, NY 10010

Produced for Windmill by Calcium Creative Ltd
Editor for Calcium Creative Ltd: Sarah Eason
US Editor: Sara Howell
Designer: Emma DeBanks

Photo credits: Cover: Shutterstock: Nate Allred. Inside: Shutterstock: 13, 15, Prasolov
Alexei 9b, Nate Allred 8, 26, Jeff Banke 27, BGSmith 4, Gina Callaway 17t, Tony
Campbell 29, James Clarke 7, Linn Currie 1, Gerald A. DeBoer 25, Dewayne Flowers
19, GG Pro Photo 17b, JPS 5, Judy Kennamer 6, Rene Kohut 23, Bruce MacQueen
24, Richard Peterson 9m, I. Pilon 20, Tom Reichner 14, Scattoselvaggio 22, Menno
Schaefer 18, Timotheos 10, Chris Turner 28, Nadezda Verbenko 9t, Visceralimage 21,
Wallenrock 11, Piotr Zajac 16, Zsschreiner 12.

Library of Congress Cataloging-in-Publication Data

Hardyman, Robyn.
Hunting / by Robyn Hardyman.
pages cm. — (Adventures in the great outdoors)
Includes index.
ISBN 978-1-61533-748-4 (library binding) — ISBN 978-1-61533-813-9 (pbk.) —
ISBN 978-1-61533-814-6 (6-pack)
1. Hunting—Juvenile literature. I. Title.
SK35.5.H37 2014
799.2—dc23

2013003811

Manufactured in the United States of America

CPSIA Compliance Information: Batch #BS13WM: For Further Information contact Windmill Books, New York, New York at 1-866-478-0556

Contents

Ready to Hunt?

Hunting is a challenging, awesome sport that brings you close to nature. There are many types of hunting, but they all require a high level of skill and a love of adventure in the great outdoors.

Whether you're looking for deer, turkeys, squirrels, or ducks, it's the thrill of the hunt that is so addictive. You're trying to outsmart a wild animal with a better knowledge of the surroundings and sharper senses than you. Hunting can be unpredictable and you may not have success for several hunts. If you treat each hunt as a challenge and a chance to learn about the animals and their environment, success will come.

A mule deer has large ears to help it detect any threats to its safety.

Safety comes first when hunting. You are using a weapon and hunting a wild animal. Think "safety first."

This wetlands habitat is ideal for hunting waterfowl.

You can hunt with a firearm or with a **crossbow**. You can hunt in woods, pastures, or wetlands. Hunting is fun both in the sunshine of spring and the snows of winter. You can hunt by day or by night. You can hunt large **game** such as elk, moose, and deer, or small game such as raccoons and squirrels. You can hunt migratory birds, game birds, or waterfowl. You need some instruction before you start to hunt, but the best training of all is experience.

Plan Your Trip

A hunting trip needs careful planning. Think about what time of year you are going and to what type of location. What will the weather be like? What qualification or license do you need to hunt in your chosen location? These are all important questions that you need to answer before you start any hunt.

All across the United States, the National Wildlife Refuge System provides incredible locations to hunt in. Look them up on the Internet. Everyone who hunts on a national wildlife refuge must have the correct state license. The license proves you have passed a firearm safety program. Refuge hunts are often organized around state hunting seasons and in line with state bagging limits. Find out about the rules in your state by contacting the state fish and game departments.

You must obey the rules when selecting a location for your hunting trip.

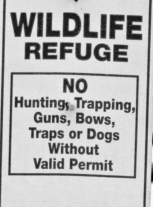

WILDLIFE REFUGE

NO
Hunting, Trapping, Guns, Bows, Traps or Dogs Without Valid Permit

Sharpen up your shooting skills before you set off.

One of the greatest hunting tools you can have is knowledge, so find out about the animal you're hunting. For example, what are its behaviors, its diet, and the best times and locations to find it? How can you track it? With answers to these questions, you'll not only hunt better, you'll also stay safe, too.

The best hunters are great **shots**, so be sure to get as much instruction and practice as you can before the season starts. You can practice on a shooting range or other safe location. Be sure to also learn the safety techniques for your firearm and how to behave safely around other hunters.

Get the Gear

If you're headed out into the wild, you need to make sure you have the right gear with you. Being properly dressed and equipped will make all the difference to the success of your hunting trip in the great outdoors.

The clothes you need depend on the time of year and the type of animals you're hunting. In winter, wear several thin layers plus a warm jacket and hat. In summer you'll need fewer layers, but a hat and a hunting jacket or vest are still a good idea. The vest has lots of pockets for holding knives, bags, and other equipment.

This hunter is properly dressed for a deer hunt.

Camouflage clothing keeps you hidden in your chosen habitat.

For many types of hunting you need **camouflage** clothes to keep you hidden as you stalk animals. The exception is deer hunting, when you must wear orange so that other hunters can see you. Keep your ammunition in a special ammo belt around your waist so you can get to it easily. Bring along a bag to hold your catch if it's small game or birds. Finally, good binoculars allow you to search for and track animals that are far away.

Binoculars are essential when searching for animals.

Guns and Bows

When you're hunting you can use a rifle, a shotgun, or a crossbow. Your choice will depend on the type of animal you're hunting, your experience, and whichever piece of equipment you personally prefer to use.

Rifles are used by many hunters. They are named for the spiraling grooves cut into the inside of the **barrel**, called rifling. These grooves make the bullet's flight more accurate. Rifles are named by caliber, which is the width of the opening in the barrel. It's very important that you use only ammunition with the same caliber as the rifle. **Cartridges** are the ammunition used in rifles. They are stored in the **magazine**. The **action** is the part of the gun that loads and fires the rifle. The stock holds the barrel and action.

Crosshairs in the rifle scope help you achieve a more accurate aim.

Hunters often attach a **scope** to their rifle. This piece of gear magnifies faraway objects and helps you to aim accurately. You must sight in your rifle before you go hunting. This means making sure the rifle and the scope are aiming at exactly the same spot.

Shotguns use **shells** as ammunition. Each shell is full of small, round pellets called shot, which **spray** out of the barrel. Shotguns are suitable for hunting small game and birds. If you're hunting big game with a shotgun you must use a solid **slug** instead. This kills large animals cleanly and humanely.

During the archery hunting season you can use a compound bow, but you need lots of practice! It's harder to hit your target with a bow and you need to be closer to the target than when using a gun.

Big Game

Tracking and hunting big game is the ultimate hunting challenge and experience. It takes time, patience, skill, and luck to bring down a large animal such as an elk, moose, or boar.

Wild boar, or hogs, live in the woods. You are more likely to see them in the evening than during the day. They come out from the cover they hide in during the day to look for food. These creatures are driven by scent, so it is possible to lure them out from their cover. A lumber post painted with creosote will attract them. You can also try corn inside a barrel. Wild boar love to eat corn!

Be careful whenever you are tracking wild boar because they can be very dangerous animals. They have sharp tusks, great strength, and a short temper.

The southern United States and the Appalachian area have the largest wild boar populations in the country.

Elk are large animals that typically weigh about 700 pounds (317 kg). They are smart animals and will leave an area if they become suspicious. The best way to attract them is by "calling" using a device called a bugle.

Always hunt elk in pairs so one hunter can call while the other sets up the shot. Just after dawn or just before dusk are the best times of day for this type of hunt. Set up your shot carefully. You'll only get one chance!

STAY SAFE! If a male elk you are stalking looks aggressive, quickly leave the area. An aggressive male can charge quickly and without notice.

Mid-September to mid-October is the best time to hunt elk, when the bulls and cows are calling to each other.

Hunting Deer

Deer hunting is one of the most popular hunting sports in the United States. White-tailed deer are found throughout much of the country, but these small and quick-footed deer can be difficult to hunt. Mule deer live in western states and are much bigger.

It is illegal to hunt female deer. However, hunting males is permitted. Male deer have **antlers** made of bone. The antlers are covered with skin and hair, called velvet. Deer can live in forests, fields, and swamps, wherever there is a supply of the plants they like to eat.

Deer are social animals that live in groups, and they communicate well with each other. If one senses trouble, it will warn the others. Deer are excellent at detecting people, by sight, by hearing, and by smell. That's why deer hunters use special scents to mask their own smells and hide away quietly as they stalk their target.

Male deer have antlers, not horns. The antlers fall off and regrow each year.

Deer Hunt

Prepare well for your deer hunt.

1 Research a location for your hunt and check the rules and regulations there.

2 Make sure you have the required licenses and permits. This can include firearm and hunting training.

3 Choose your weapon. There are different seasons for using bows and firearms, so check this out. Choose between a rifle and a shotgun, and prepare the weapon and ammunition. Most deer hunters use rifles.

4 Find the orange clothing required for your area. Most states specify how much orange must be worn. This is to protect you from other hunters.

5 Collect warm clothing, including a hat, gloves, and strong boots.

You will need:

- licenses and permits
- clothing in hunter orange
- warm clothing
- weapon and ammunition

This hunter is wearing hunter orange and warm clothing for his deer hunt.

Deer Success

You're all set and you've headed out before dawn so that you can get into the best position for your hunt. Choose this position carefully. It is key to making your hunt successful.

First, you need to stake out a place to lie in wait for deer, using your knowledge of their behavior. Look for signs of the deer, such as tracks, droppings, or paths through the grass or woodland. Think about where the deer might come to find water and food.

Many hunters position themselves on a **blind**, or wooden shelter built on a raised platform. This gives them a good, hidden viewing point.

STAY SAFE! Always keep your rifle's safety on until you are ready to fire.

A blind hides you and your scent from the deer and gives you a good view.

Get in position before the
Sun comes up.

Ideally you should get in position before dawn, as the deer will come out to feed as the Sun comes up. Do not shoot until the light is good enough to see properly. Once in position, keep still and silent.

If you're using a rifle, use the scope to get a good fix on the deer. If you're using a bow, you'll need to get closer, in silence.

Choose whether to use a rifle with cartridges, or a shotgun with slugs. Never use shells with shot for a deer.

17

Small Game

When you're starting out in the sport of hunting, you'll find it easier to hunt small game. Up in the trees you'll find gray squirrels and fox squirrels.

In the United States there are two main types of squirrel. Fox squirrels have a rust-red coat and gray squirrels are gray. Fox squirrels are an easier target because their color stands out more than that of gray squirrels.

Squirrels like to nest in hardwood trees, such as oak. Look for piles of nut casings or pinecones at the foot of a tree, or droppings. You'll be sure to see the squirrels scurrying up and down the trees.

STAY SAFE!

Always keep a look out for other hunters around you. Squirrel hunting is popular at certain times of year.

Fox squirrels are easier to see in the trees than gray squirrels.

Cook your Catch

Make the most of your catch. Squirrel meat tastes great when it's braised slowly.

1 Remove the squirrel pieces from the brine, pat dry, and coat in seasoned flour.

2 Heat the oil in an ovenproof casserole dish and brown the squirrel pieces in batches, then remove them.

3 Add the broth to the casserole dish and bring it to a boil.

4 Add the chopped chili, garlic, olives, and almonds, and stir well.

5 Put the squirrel back in the pot, cover, and cook in the oven for around 1 ½ hours.

Explore This!

You will need, for 4 people:

• 3 squirrels, skinned, gutted, and cut into pieces. Soak them for 6 hours in a brine solution with bay leaves and thyme.

• ½ cup of flour seasoned with salt and pepper

• salt and pepper

• ¼ cup chopped almonds

• 3 finely chopped cloves of garlic

• 1 cup pitted and sliced green olives

• olive oil

• 1 finely chopped onion

• 1 finely chopped small chili

• 1 cup chicken broth

A shotgun is the usual weapon for hunting squirrels, although you can also use a rifle.

Game on the Ground

Hunters love hunting rabbits, hares, and other small game because it can be straightforward and easy to catch lots of these animals.

Rabbits and hares eat grasses and other vegetation, and you'll find them just about anywhere those are in a good supply. They tend to stay close to home, too, so if you see one, it's likely there are plenty more of them around.

Raccoons are nocturnal, which means they mostly come out at night. If you are hunting them you'll have the most success at dusk and beyond. To hunt them you need a good light and a hunting dog to retrieve your raccoon. You also need to scout the area well, as the raccoons will cover a lot of ground, fast!

Raccoons are good swimmers and great at climbing, so be ready for the chase.

Coyote Hunt

If you're ready for a bigger challenge, you could try a coyote hunt.

1 Choose your clothing. If it's snowy, camouflage yourself in white clothes.

2 Apply a scent that masks your human scent. Coyotes have an incredible sense of smell to help them find prey.

3 Scout your hunting area to find a good spot.

4 Use a call to attract the coyote, such as one that mimics a rabbit in distress.

5 Use your binoculars to search for a target.

6 Don't move around because coyotes will sense you. Stay in one place.

You will need:

- gun that works well close to a target
- warm clothing, white if it's snowy
- scent to mask your own
- binoculars
- a call

Coyotes have excellent senses, so you have to be smart when hunting them.

Hunting Birds

Upland game birds include quail, pheasant, and grouse. People also target waterfowl such as ducks, and migratory birds, such as woodcock and snipe when hunting birds.

Upland game bird hunting is mostly about walking to find the birds. Walk through the habitat that your chosen bird prefers. Ruffed grouse are often found where two habitats meet, such as meadow and woodland. They're also attracted to streams and areas with berries. California quail favor brush.

When hunting waterfowl, there are several techniques to use. You can flush out a group of birds with a dog and shoot once they fly up, or you can use **decoys**.

STAY SAFE!

Always be sure you know what is in front of your target and beyond it before you pull the trigger.

Ringneck pheasants can be found in the grasslands of northern California.

using Decoys

Try hunting waterfowl with decoys.

1 Decoys are made to look like the birds you are hunting. Place them in a location favored by your target.

2 Set your blind no more than 40 yards (36 m) away, with the wind coming from behind you. Birds land into the wind.

3 Ensure there is an open area of land in front of you for the birds to land on.

4 When the birds circle over the decoys, making sure it is safe to land, you can identify them.

5 As the birds come into land, take aim. The law says you must use nontoxic shot.

6 Use your dog to retrieve the birds, especially from the water.

You will need:

- shotgun with shells of nontoxic shot
- camouflage clothing
- dog for retrieving birds
- 6 or more decoys
- portable blind (optional)

Decoy geese attract birds to within the hunter's range.

A Turkey Hunt

Millions of people in the United States hunt wild turkeys. The sport is so popular because tracking and bringing down one of these amazing birds is quite a challenge.

Wild turkeys are big birds! They can weigh more than 20 pounds (9 kg). The birds are found in many habitats, from grasslands and woods to swamps and chaparral, but they mainly live in forests. Wild turkeys eat both plants and insects.

Gobblers are larger and more colorful than female turkeys.

The larger a turkey's beard, the more prized it is among hunters.

It's often illegal to hunt female turkeys, called hens, or chicks. Male turkeys are called gobblers and most states usually allow them to be hunted. Always check the rules of your state, however.

Gobblers have a beard, which is a bristly area of feathers on their breast that can be 10–21 inches (25–53 cm) long. They also have a spur, which is a long claw on their back leg. Both the beard and claw get bigger as the turkey gets older. You can tell if a turkey is a prized "trophy" by the size of its beard and spur.

Turkey hunting takes place in fall, winter, and spring. In spring and summer turkeys eat insects, berries, green leaves, and grass seeds. In fall and winter they eat acorns and the fruit on trees such as maple, ash, pine, and beech. Some hunters think it is more of a challenge to hunt turkeys in the fall, because at this time of year it's harder to get the birds to come toward you.

Turkey Success

Never try to sneak up on a turkey! It's not safe because you could be shot accidentally by another hunter. It's also likely that the turkey will see and hear you. Successful turkey hunting is all about scouting, sitting, and waiting.

Scout your hunting area well in advance. Choose the turkeys' favored habitat and look for signs of the birds, such as feathers, tracks in wet dirt or sand, and scratches on the ground where they've looked for food. Choose a good place to sit and wait, such as a broad tree you can lean against. This hides your outline. You need the birds to come to you, and to shoot you must be within around 40 yards (36 m) of them.

These turkey hunters are using bows instead of shotguns.

STAY SAFE! If you're using decoys, always cover them when you carry them, so other hunters don't shoot at them!

If you are patient when turkey hunting you can have great success.

Turkey hunters use a shotgun with shells of shot, or a bow. Using a bow takes great skill because it's harder to get an accurate aim and you must get even closer to the bird than you would if using a gun.

You must wear camouflage because turkeys can detect colors, including orange. Cover your head, hands, and face if possible. You can use decoys and calls to attract the turkeys.

Go Green

We all have a responsibility to keep our wild places safe and unspoiled for the future. That way, everyone can continue to enjoy them. Whatever your outdoor adventure, remember to respect the natural environment and make as little impact on it as you can.

If hunters are to be successful in a hunt, they must know and understand the natural world well. They also have to respect their environment or they will not have much success. On trips to scout a location, whether it's the forest, the grasslands, or the wetlands, don't disturb what you find. Make your impact as small as possible and, when your hunting day is over, always take all your equipment and your litter home with you. Piles of shot from shells can be extremely dangerous to some animals, even fatal, if they eat it.

Respect hunting laws regarding the number of animals you can catch.

Learn as much as you can about the natural world and the animals within it.

Hunting laws aim to protect animal populations. They control the times of year when you can hunt and limit the number of animals you can catch. It's essential that you respect these limits and obey the rules. Never bag more than your allowance. Why not help to protect the habitats and animals you love by joining a conservation organization in your area? The work they do ensures the healthy survival of wild animals for everyone in the future.

Glossary

action (AK-shun) The part of a rifle that loads and fires it.

antlers (ANT-lerz) Long growths on the heads of deer, made of bone and covered with skin and hair. They fall off and regrow each year.

barrel (BAR-ul) The long, hollow part of a gun through which the shot is fired.

blind (BLYND) A shelter or screen that hides a hunter from his prey.

camouflage (KA-muh-flahj) A pattern, often on clothing, that is used to hide someone or something in its surroundings.

cartridges (KAR-trij-ez) The ammunition used with a rifle.

crossbow (KROS-boh) A weapon used for hunting that uses a tight string to fire arrows as ammunition.

decoys (DEE-koyz) Imitation birds or other animals used to attract prey during a hunt.

game (GAYM) An animal that is hunted for sport or food.

magazine (MA-guh-zeen) The part of a gun that holds the ammunition.

rifle (RY-ful) A gun with spiral grooves cut into the barrel.

scope (SKOHP) A device used with a rifle that magnifies faraway objects and helps to improve aim.

shells (SHELZ) Metal containers for ammunition that are loaded into a shotgun. A shell can contain shot or a solid slug.

shots (SHOTZ) Small metal pellets fired from shotguns.

shotgun (SHOT-gun) A gun used for firing at close range.

slug (SLUG) Solid ammunition that is fired from a shotgun.

spray (SPRAY) To spread out across an area.

Further Reading

Chandler, Matt. *Deer Hunting for Kids*. Into the Great
Outdoors. Mankato, MN: Capstone Press, 2013.

Lambert, Hines. *Hunting Turkeys*. Let's Go Hunting.
New York: PowerKids Press, 2013.

MacRae, Sloan. *Small-Game Hunting: Rabbits,
Squirrels, and Other Small Animals*. Open Season.
New York: PowerKids Press, 2011.

Websites

For web resources related to the subject of this book, go to:
www.windmillbooks.com/weblinks and select this book's title.

Index

B
big game, 11–13
blinds, 16, 23

C
calibers, 10
camouflage, 9, 21, 23
cartridges, 10, 17
coyotes, 21

D
decoys, 22–23, 27
deer, 4–5, 8–9, 14–17

E
elk, 5, 12–13
equipment, 5, 8–11, 15–17, 19,
  21, 23, 26–28

G
game birds, 5, 22
grouse, 22

H
hares, 20

M
mule deer, 4, 14

P
permits, 15
pheasants, 22

Q
quail, 22

R
rabbits, 20–21
raccoons, 5, 20

S
small game, 5, 9, 11, 18–20
squirrels, 4–5, 18–19

T
turkeys, 4, 24–27

W
waterfowl, 5, 22–23
white-tailed deer, 14
wild boar, 12